The Disappearing Poet Blues

The Bucknell Series in Contemporary Poetry

This is one of a limited number of books of poetry of the highest quality published annually by the Bucknell University Press, in conjunction with *West Branch Library Journal* and the Stadler Center for Poetry.

Titles in This Series

Karl Patten, *Touch*
Afaa Weaver, *The Ten Lights of God*
Charles Borkhuis, *Alpha Ruins*
Harryette Mullen, *Tree Tall Woman*
Katherine Soniat, *Alluvial*
Floyd Skloot, *The Fiddler's Trance*
Marc Hudson, *The Disappearing Poet Blues*

http://www.departments.bucknell.edu/univ_press

The Disappearing Poet Blues

Marc Hudson

Lewisburg
Bucknell University Press
London: Associated University Presses

Associated University Presses
440 Forsgate Drive
Cranbury, NJ 08512

Associated University Presses
16 Barter Street
London WC1A 2AH, England

Associated University Presses
P.O. Box 338, Port Credit
Mississauga, Ontario
Canada L5G 4L8

The paper used in this publication meets the requirements of the American National Standard for Permanence of Paper for Printed Library Materials Z39.48-1984.

Library of Congress Cataloging-in-Publication Data

Hudson, Marc, 1947–
The disappearing poet blues / Marc Hudson.
p. cm.—(Bucknell series in contemporary poetry)
ISBN 0-8387-5506-2 (alk. paper)
I. Title. II. Series.

PS3558.U3114 D5 2002
811′.54—dc21 2001037759

PRINTED IN THE UNITED STATES OF AMERICA

for the comitatus,
Helen, Ian, and Alix

Love? What is It? Most natural painkiller.
What there is. LOVE.

—William S. Burroughs
Final Journal Entry

Contents

In the Middle of Life

Coda

Acknowledgments

Grateful acknowledgement is due the editors of the following magazines in which some of these poems first appeared:

Arts Indiana: "Our Son the Cosmonaut," "Archaeology," and "The Archer"
Fine Madness: "At Culver Hospital," "Dry Landscape at Easter-Time," and "Walt Whitman at the Patent House"
The Flying Island: "After a Painting by Diego Rivera"
The Hopewell Review: "Deliberation" and "A Familiar Song"
Indiannual 5: "Aubade"
The Kenyon Review: "An Icelandic Door"
Madison Review: "A Little While Ago"
The Massachusetts Review: "A Monk on Heimaey"
Mississippi Mud: "Caedmon"
Paper Boat: "Okanogan String Band Music"
Poetry East: "Bathing Ian" and "By Indian River, Baranof Island"
Prairie Schooner: "The Human City," "After a Line by Antonio Machado," "Grace," and "The Project"
The Sewanee Review: "Wiglaf's Tale," "Doxology at Glacier Bay," "To an Actor Friend at 44," and "Musée de Vieux Salauds"
Tar River Poetry: "Dr. Latham's Photographs"
"Wiglaf's Tale" was first published in the *Sewanee Review,* vol. 94, no. 3, Summer 1986. Copyright by Marc Hudson.
"To an Actor Friend at 44" was first published in the *Sewanee Review,* vol. 104, no. 4, Fall 1996. Copyright by Marc Hudson.
"Doxology at Glacier Bay" and "Musée de Vieux Salauds" were first published in the *Sewanee Review,* vol. 105, no. 4, Fall 1997. Copyright by Marc Hudson.

Grateful acknowledgment is made to the Grove Press of Grove-Atlantic for permission to reprint an excerpt from *Last Words: the Final Journals of William S. Burroughs,* edited by James Grauerholz. Copyright 2001 by William S. Burroughs Trust.

I would like to express my gratitude to the National Endowment for the Arts, to the Yaddo Foundation, to the Island Institute, and to Wabash College for support during the time some of these poems were written. Thanks also are due to friends and fellow writers, James Snydal, Richard Blackburn, Sam Green, Bert Stern, Tam Lin Neville, Alice Friman, and Cynthia Hogue; to my beloved teachers, Leslie Norris and Nelson Bentley; to the keen-eyed editors, George Core and Hilda Raz; and to my most ardent reader and critic, Helen Mundy Hudson, my wife, partner, and pal, loving thanks.

The Disappearing Poet Blues

Nespelem

The Disappearing Poet Blues

Pretty soon now and I'll begin my journey,
throw my rucksack in the back of the VW,
my dog-eared edition of *The Narrow Road*
to the Deep North. I'll put on my old ankh
with its black leather thong, and, in my jeans
pocket, for good luck, a sea-worn green
stone. Before I go, I'll pause
in the hallway outside my children's rooms—
Ian's breathing more soft than the susurrus
of his feeding pump, dripping the Jevity
through his stoma; Alix, more restless,
murmuring something about a raccoon.
I will kiss them each, once, graze the lips
of Helen the strong, the exhausted, then slip
through the back door out of town. I will not
stop to board the eastbound train like Ezra—
Venice and Rapallo are not on my itinerary.
I will head west. West where the heroes always vanish,
where the derelict fathers go mad in Missoula.
West with the runaways to the endless reservations
of sky and pine and red moon rising through mesquite.
I've rehearsed it all, the tao of self-erasure.
Past Culver Hospital, I'll take the west on-ramp
as other fathers have, their wheels spinning
out of control on the soft shoulders of their lives.
Flooring the accelerator, I'll merge with the eighteen wheelers
hauling their loads of coke and livestock, their pig-iron and
  plutonium
cores from the aging reactors.
I will make good my escape from the Old Jail
Museum and the stone tablet sarcophagi
of Monday afternoon faculty meetings.
Gone from this "godforsaken desert beanery,"
plunging west over the Wabash, the Vermilion,
the dirty Illinois, the dawn at my back,
the clamor of my children starting to waken
as I cross the Big Muddy, equator of our country,
on the cusp of the Millennium. I'm bailing out,

I got the disappearing poet blues
like Ez and Jack and nameless other professors
of oblivion jazz, deadbeat dads blowing the riffs
of their guilt-trips over the malls of Middle America.
I seek a comitatus, a silence so deep
you could call it death or just living in paranoia,
Montana, in a windowless shack, in the shadow of a satellite
disc, in the cross-hairs of an FBI sniper, scribbling
ecological tracts against the American empire
or plotting the demolition of the Capitol
with a well-lobbed zen koan. I cross the line
near Sundance into the windy rectangle that is Wyoming.
East is pollen-yellow, north the Devil's Tower,
clawed stub of our shattered axle-tree.
Ah, father basalt, old thumb, are you hitching a ride
with me this morning, seeking new orogenies,
more adventitious species still to unfold from the hidden
strata? I share your sediments completely.
A mountain climbs me as I dream west from Indiana
toward the tree-line and the cinquefoil sky-mind
of pater noster lakes under snow peaks.
West of Still Water and Sweet Grass, the wind flames
green—*Verde, verde que te quiero verde* I chant Lorca
under my breath. Montana's motto is "Oro y Plata."
Miners still bank on it, scouring the ridges like Nazi dentists.
At Anaconda, you need a lot of Novocain
to look out your windshield and not see heartbreak.
On the Continental Divide, Chief Joseph's tears
poured east and west. He gave our blue coats the slip,
he almost made the border, but compassion
for the children held him back and he was captured.
Now spotted napweed cloaks the Lolo valleys,
the damaged lands all lavender cattle can't eat.
I cross the Garnet Range, the Bitterroots,
the old compulsion reeling me back through Idaho
Spokane the Channeled Scablands Coulee Dam Electric
City Omak—I am helpless to resist the pull
back to the middens of salmon bones and charred
juniper, the locked waters behind Chief Joseph
Dam. I cannot release them, unless the poem

were a form of astral projection, unless it could whisper
to an inattentive doctor, a midwife of more than memory.

Always now, I'm driving through the western night,
past the blurred signs, the spiral curves of petroglyphs,
as my zig-zagging Beetle eats the miles between this moment
and my lost Okanogan.

A Father Born
July 1983

My fatherhood began,
a kind of salvage operation.

In Nespelem,
in the field museum
of the archaeology project,
among chert points and stone pestles,
the charred pollens of a thousand years,
I took the call from Spokane—

a doctor—Bodenstein?—
saying, "Dad, your son
is dying." "Dad" I was christened—
that father not yet a father
of a few hours, of a baby
seizing under a ventilator,
his lungs filling with fluid.

A river had been secretly rising
all those months,
creeping over sandbars,
undercutting banks
where cliff swallows build.

Those dry hills were his,
those glacier-cut, waterless
canyons were my son's.
And the high valleys of sweet grass
along the San Poil, yarrow,
mullein, bitterroot: a people's
history. They were his
natal country now, the place
of my paternity.

Late July, then August
he lay under the ventilator,
hardly stirring. In Omak,

these were festival days.
Boys raced their ponies
down a cutbank, then across
the Okanogan. Now I understood
their ritual leap to mend
a broken life. I had been
a curator of bones;
now I was the father
of a small church made of them.

Deliberation

When the doctors told me you might not have a mind,
I thought of all those fathers
who carried their babies up into the mountains

and imagined carrying you through that grove of cottonwoods
at the mouth of Panama Canyon
and, higher, through airy tracts of ponderosa
where the soil is a bronze fragrance of fallen needles
until we emerge in the clear light
under a cliff face. I would kneel and kiss
your forehead and lay you in your purple blanket
in the talus, in the frost of early evening,
asleep.

So those fathers took care of their own.
There was no place for a boy
such as you, no place at the fire
for a twisted one. And the father, I suppose,
made the decision.

Often, in those first months of your life,
I would lift you up in my arms
to weigh who you were
and the monster I might become.
Then, slowly, deliberately,
as if calibrating a moral instrument,
I would lower you back into your crib.
I would tuck the comforter around your shoulders,
very carefully I would kiss your forehead.

First Milk

You propped his picture on your lap
and gazed at it to bring down
your milk, the first milk
rich in colostrum
and unknown immunogens.
The doctor had written
a prescription to dry up your milk,
but you wadded it up and pumped,
studying the picture the Lifebird
nurse had snapped: our six-
hour-old son, wired at chest
and wrist, skinny as that monkey
named Abel they shot into space
in an Atlas nosecone. I can't
remember if he ever came down.
Our son, at least, survived
his copter ride to Sacred Heart,
though the doctors spoke in parables
of babies whose living parents
orphan them. Turning your face
to his picture, you expressed
your sweet milk, which we sealed
in plastic bags and packed in dry ice
against the blaze of August.

If anything saved Ian,
it was your milk, Helen,
the beistings thick as cream
and full of mysterious power
as any potion and your stubborn,
continuous pumping, gazing
constantly at our son.

Our Son the Cosmonaut

Strapped in his black chair with the velcro thongs,
webbed & buckled at shoulder & waist
and linked via head-switch to the Mac's scanning mode,
he is like Yuri Gagarin riding his flimsy capsule
into the void, or that Apollo crew
after the oxygen tank explodes
& they clamber aboard the lunar module—
there to watch while the moon,
beautiful as a wheel of Gorgonzola,
drifts beyond their grasp forever.

And when his lift clangs down & he descends
to the Waffle House of Dothan, Alabama,
he's the alien from Arcturus, the silent ambassador
of the Holothurians, the silica creature
in its exoskeleton, *Homo metallicus*.
Evangelists mob him, barking in tongues,
old women in crumpled housecoats shuffle past
dropping twenty dollar bills in his lap,
while parents cluck at their children
& their children continue to stare in spoon-halted wonder.

At his birth, trim & smiling personnel
in fawnbrown flightsuits descended on Omak,
they pricked him & snipped him & took his pulse,
they taped electrodes to his chest & waist.
They said he was "bicycling" & shot him full
of strontium & Geritol, "just in case,"
then bagged him & wired him & shunted him
by copter to the Mother Ship.

There they kept him in a hydroponic garden
bathed in glucose & pure O_2
& Stuckey said he would do just fine
but Maixner shook his head.
Then they took us on a tour of discarded suns,
of wan bubbles of matter & entropy's wilderness.
They lectured us on "Seal Physiology & the Diving Reflex,"

on “Brains That Resemble Swiss Cheese”
& on “The Care & Feeding of Infantile Spasms.”
When we returned, if it was to Earth, it was an Earth
invisibly altered, we & our son were changelings,
or the very grass was, its molecules all sinister.
At the exit threshold, one with her face cast down
placed in our hands a precious vial
of anti-stigmata skin cream.

These many years & he is still orbiting
parsecs beyond the faintest comet, where the spectra
of migrant stars are most red.
We need nanotechnology & laser X-rays,
we need Richard Feynman drumming a samba
while he scribbles the equation for a neuron switch,
we need the radars of NORAD plus Watson & Crick
to plot his Doppler Shift, to get a fix
on his true position.

And still we dream of him ascending, as if weightless,
from his chair, his perfect body untethered at last,
free of thoracic pads & bivalve casts, the boy himself
tottering toward us, admonishing our tears.

Dr. Latham's Photographs

"Joseph's Band of *Nez Perces* reside in the Nespelem Valley. . . .
They are not industrious. Their moral and sanitary condition is
not good. They profess no religion."

—Report of Physician at Colville Agency, Edward Latham,
Nespelem, Washington, July 15, 1892

1

Nespelem is a couple of clapboard shacks
beyond a crowded waste of mullein.
No barbed wire, only wind and crumbling ridges.
No turrets, no guard towers but the far mountains
lost in haze. History has dumped them here—
the Columbias, the Cayuse, the proud Nez Perce—
in this empty land of cheat grass and scattered yellow pine,
these folds of dry hills like faded khaki.

2

Latham paid Chief Joseph five bucks
plus two sacks of potatoes to pose him there
by the flashing river. Late fall, 1903:
all but thirty years since Joseph withdrew
into the mountains with his people,
disappearing into Montana, as if several hundred
women, children, pack mules and dogs
had become streaming mist in the Lolo forests.
Now, bowlegged, fleshy, he
uselessly grips the prop of a Winchester,
his sidelong glance a hatchet.
A strong wind whips his war bonnet,
his mouth is set. The Nespelem earth
looks bone-dry, the cottonwoods, the shore brush,
bare of leaf. Nondescript in their strangeness,
the seasons of exile.

3

And here's Swan Woman, Joseph's aunt
whom the whites call Old Jean.

She fought all through the '77 Campaign,
hiding her dead in talus and willow brush
so the soldiers couldn't tally the bodies.
Staggering under a load of brush and an axe,
she squints at Latham. Behind her,
half-visible, a wagon track,
a treeless ridge with gray outcrops.
Two daughters and five sons
are buried in Idaho. Beside her white braids,
bright strings of beads hang down.

4

One by one, Latham collects them—
Yellow Bull, Chief Moses of the Columbias,
Charlie Wilpocken and his gentle wife, Kill-es-tum,
the shaman Quiotsa. Their beautiful faces
seem denuded as the drab hills.
Their flower-patterned beaded vests,
their Pendleton blankets and dentalium
necklaces hang as if on mannequins
at the Smithsonian. Even the babies
laced into cradleboards dangle from trees
like pupae. He takes their pictures
the way our fathers took their lands—
a wink, a flick of the wrist
and the shutter drops, a landscape changes
hands. Magic paper draws to itself
the sacked ranges, impounding
the swift waters and tulle lakes of the Wallowas,
basins quaking with buffalo grass.
They freeze before his camera
as if it were a kill jar.

5

He has no salve for exile,
knows nothing of the lore of roots—
yarrow—"chipmunk's tail"—
for binding wounds, water cress
to cool a fever, wild carrot

for thrush. The tribal women
distrust him, keep him far
from any birth. His medicine
is all placebo, useless
against disbelief. He must
oversee a vague, wasting malady.
His sole competence
is the witness of loss.

A Little While Ago

She was playing by the river

Women were pounding camas roots with heavy cobbles
A rattler sunned on a stone

A little while ago
a boy could find his way
up the canyon choked with hackberry
over scree, the dry flume of a creekbed
to the flame-shaped darkness of larches

A little while ago
men left arrows of red ocher
on spalled rock
went elsewhere

Old women, their spines crooked
as the hawthorn, had eyes
like children who first see
the just-risen moon
Camping by the river
they built sweet fires of sage and juniper

They found her there
a clean-limbed child
her breast-buds
scarlet as the currant berry
wearing the bright water like anklets

That was the month of snowmelt
the serviceberry soon to cascade
in whiteness everywhere

a little while ago
she sang and it was time
to dig the wild onion

Dry Landscape at Easter-Time
April 1984

Off and on for weeks now, soft rain. Serviceberry blooms
in the cliff-scree, white puffs and huddles against the moss-green
ridge: our dry country dogwood. Bunchgrass and yarrow
sprout on the river bench. Sage is redolent—a slight pressure
on that blue-silver leaf yields a serious odor, not unpleasant.

Driving back from Coulee Dam, today I took the Buffalo Lake road.
Below, to the left, lay the drowned river
with its glare of neglected pewter, and the abrupt
rise to the basalt rim, a rugged garden at its base
of hackbrush, syringa, pale-leafed aspen. It seemed

right to come this route in the late afternoon of Good Friday,
to stop by the cliff face and watch a cloud of swallows
clinging to the rock, then dropping back into the air—
the broken country scored with blossoms, the avid birds
jabbing the stone for purchase, and on it all a late bronze
light, a slow pulsation—the landscape still transfigured
in the absence of Christ.

Archaeology
July 1994

Nothing of us remains
except the rock piles
that propped the trailers, the volunteer
sunflowers where your garden was.
What should we expect after ten years?
Place has its own preoccupations.
People who lived here centuries
are the dust we breathe.

In grief, I threw myself into the snow
to blot it out—the CAT scans
and anticonvulsants, our infant
son twitching like a pithed frog—,
to finally pull the plug
on this dolorous machine.
My robot of a body
carried me over that winter.
Dry hills remembered how to flower,
exorbitant blossoms of arrowleaf,
and the child's seizures stopped.
For a few weeks, we could trust
the April sun, the south wind
loud with meadowlarks. Summer
hammered us with the truth.

Naive to think place should remember.
No ash or iridium, no slivers of obsidian
mark those months.
That a child suffered here,
a mother and a father knew grief,
is etched into nothing
except our faces.

Northern Interlude

Doxology at Glacier Bay

Did He say to the kittiwakes,
"Hunger and be beautiful,
sweep down and take the krill
on avid parabolas"?
And to the pollens of the cottonwoods,
"Be pungent, my sweet ones,
lightly float across the Bay
and service the far receptacles"?
And what was on His mind
when He flung the waterfalls
down the cirques and evolved
the narwhal's tusk? Did He know
what He was doing
when He cut those cliffs
and thrust green embers
under the ice? Was He lucid
when He made so much light?
Did He foresee such beauty
could be worth a slow crucifixion?

Wiglaf's Tale

"... harp music
shall not wake the warrior, but the black raven
over the soon-to-die shall caw merrily ..."

—*Beowulf*

Why should I speak? He foretold it all,
the horseman on the cliff, said we would wake
in the cold dawn with ravens cawing,
the harp forgotten. I sat with a king
broken in my arms, the sun guttering
on stone pillars. All was heavy,
death-leaden—the daggered fire-drake,
its torques of useless gold, like braided tresses
of a young girl. And my kinsmen
approaching from the holt, hangdog
in their dishonor, huskmen already
eviscerate of time as the quelled dragon.
I raged at them, but now would not.
They have been cut and bundled away,
spear-winnowed, and gold torn
from their throats.
What more is there to say?
A life of sorts, such rags and scraps
as memory keeps. Time has put the torch
to everything else. One truth I'll tell you:
in a strange house, keep your own counsel.
And another: the dead are as prone to lie
as the living. Bodies of sawdust,
fingers and jaws worked by strings,
who speaks for them?
Our king's ashes
were scarcely cold when Eadgils comes,
a grey cur on the track of carrion.
We sent him home, his tail between his legs,
his two whelps staked to the tideland,
outshouting the waves. How they begged
a better death, cursing us at the last.
They might have saved their breath.

The warm south greened the fells,
brought whimbrel and godwit to haunt
our fields, and Frisians ghosting landward
on a calm bay. They took us quickly,
too many, too swift, sea-crows hurtling
in a red fog. Clothed only in wounds,
I woke, a light, sweet shower
glinting on boulder and grass. Like worms
drowned in the rain, my slaughtered kinsmen,
and the ravens, black robins, hopping
among them. I wanted nothing but to follow;
my good blood barred the way.

I took ship, shoved out, with the handful
who, like me, half-lived. Of that departure
I remember only the gulls, their keening
hard to bear because it held no grief.
Later, I thought of our king—he and Breca
in the coils of the flood, his voyage to Denmark,
sad Hrothgar, the cleansing of the blood-bright hall:
a grey sea makes an easy glass
for the dreaming mind. That was our dawn
and I was born to our tribe's evening,
my hand knobbed and cautered by dragon-fire.
If I shut my eyes, I could see our kindred
like a long branch severed from a shore-tree
and floating out, green needles replaced
by dragging weed, raw wood clenched
by barnacles, finger-joints of the clutching sea.
And I remember (better than I saw)
whales gliding on the fallow waves,
mowing them like men with sickles.
Gannets fell from the clouds to glean
the ruddy gobbets. I passed a hand
over my eyes. Next I remember
a plug of rock, perfect columns
a mason must have shaped, there in the dead middle
of the way to Thule. Dawn, the tenth day,
an island cut the horizon, a green headland
webbed with white strings of waterfalls.

Fulmars bobbed in the backwash, cormorants
treaded the water, trying to gain
the air, and again the wild mockery
of the black-backed gulls. But the green promontory,
the braiding, milk-white becks drew me.
I kissed my brother, laid the sword
of Weohstan across his lap,
the snake-adorned blade, said, "Use it well."
Then dove into the sliding, flesh-annealing
darkness, swam far in the soundless
holts of kelp, where fisherbirds harry
the streaming capelin. And surfaced, blowing,
my teeth clattering, took aim
for a crescent beach under green blades
of sea and grass.
                    Where the fresh island stream
fanned through gravel and bird-tracked bay mud
I woke later, idly watched
nameless grey birds dashing in and out
of the surf, a redshank prising open
a mussel shell: the same play
I'd seen before, the same taking of flesh
and atonement, as when the dragon branded
my king, and was taxed in turn for its avidity.
Feathered and fingered, the sea encumbers
the creatures with its several hungers.

I lived among the rocks, their sulfur and russet
lichen, on the eggs of seabirds, small
herbs, whatever. Another came after awhile,
heaped a beehive-shaped barrow,
and took me for the poor spirit of that place.
I showed him freshets and edible mosses;
he taught me Latin and the Fall of Rome.
I spoke of Ingeld and he of Christ,
the young champion mounting the Cross,
the endless dispensing of his body. Then I learned
how the world has been fastened on vellum, the earth
chained in a book; and almost killed him
but for his sheepish courtesy, his willingness to die.

He made sweet songs for all hours,
but his eye was elsewhere, captured by that radiant
cloud, the late cloud that commands the eye
when night overtakes all else. I preferred
rotten stone, pocked tufa
to his Plotinus. But we got on,
brother exiles on our bird island.
He recited Augustine, I sang of Sigemund
and my Beowulf: he listened all
one twi-lit night, the kittiwakes silent,
the sea a banked fire off to the south.
When I had finished, he muttered "Heorot"
under his breath, and the name fixed itself
to the sea there, burning.
A ship came,
more of Christ's folk, and I left the island
at my friend's urging, to pilot their sealskin
basket south. I crewed on other ships—
from Carthage to Rome and Byzantium,
with wheat in the hold or green amphorae
of African wine. Eleusis, Delos,
Jerusalem: I saw the blood-rimmed
rocks, like milling stones, whereon
we grind our gods. And at dawn once
while two larks swerved about a headland's
wind-broken pine, clamorous, innocent
of everything but their little desire,
I saw two navies engage and grapple
like great saurians, nickers risen
from the muddy sea-bottom, heard the groan
of wrenched keelsons, the confused cries
of those in chains smothered below
while those above could at least choose
between spear and fire and the salt flood.
Lying in the sweet pungence of yarrow,
I saw it all. And two birds
with yellow gorgets fluttered and chirped
as if our kind had vanished from the world.

I, Wiglaf, Weohstan's son,
have seen these things, nor pretend wisdom,

that map of a shattered archipelago
my king once had by heart. Call me a witness,
a childless memory. Some branches sing
when you put them in the fire. Say I was one.

Caedmon

So the angel said, "Sing, Caedmon,
of Genesis." The Word had spoken
among staring beastheads
and damp straw, as it had
seven centuries before.
Like any beast, he chafed
under that burden
of articulate sound,
the tongue-tied mucker of stalls,
the silent one.
                    But there it was—
a man in harness to the creatures themselves,
a lowly form mired in fear,
singing. For Hild the abbess
and the lettered clerics,
the miracle couldn't be more—
as if worm and maggot,
the eyeless cattle of the earth,
and fawn-capped coprophiles
whose mycelia thread the dung,
even infusoria in muddy troughs,
paramecia—as if these were singing,
the motes of homesick light
finding their way to praise.

A Monk on Heimaey

The long hours sift me.
Years ago, I set aside my life
as a courtesy to silence.
I came to the seal's ledge, the warm, still-forming
island with its strange horns of terra cotta.
I let history go, Caesar and Cassiodorus,
even the Phoenix-adorned Gospels were too garish.
Limpets became my scribes, scurs and flaws
of ice, lichen, their mindless acids.
They labor in the endless scriptorium
incising rock with a Latin Lucretius would approve.

So I learn to savor
the beautiful incompleteness of the terrene—
rock weathers and therein roots a green randomness.
But for Him, the voyager on his spar,
who is my home and harbor.

Reports of the outer world sometimes intrude.
An eyeless doll washes up in the kelp,
fires smudge the horizon, ash
falls on my cabbages. I brush it off.
For the puffins return to their green porches
bearded with fingerlings. They graze beyond
the breakers.

I no longer grieve to hear the gulls,
nor laugh with the fulmars. I am grown cold
with the power of rock, the brandished cup
of Ocean. All I keep is an image of Christ
with his great seafaring eyes, O Salvator Mundi!
and these white ledges sharp against my knees.

An Icelandic Door
In Memoriam Paul Skoog (1903–82)

1

He carved this door
as a pilgrim would undertake
a long penance—silent, hooded
in rough serge, take ship

the sea in his nostrils
like the blood he owed God.

Mindful of those
foundered on ledges
for whom landfall
was a falling away
from human memory,

and of those compassless in fog
turning toward the unseen
rock, their strakes soon broken,
keel and keelson crushed
and all loveliness
of leaf-carved and tendril-like coiling
prowstem,

he rubbed the blade
back and forth
on lava stone.

Then asked that his hands
not move
until the shadows of the grasses
and the shadows of the floating seabirds
fade from the wall,
and he saw
only the story
telling itself on the empty
roundels of the door.

2

For Paul Skoog, I call up
an image of that carver—
a grey-eyed man of seventy—
and set him to work
on the great roundel, the elaborate coils
of the world-engirdling dragon.

Again, at Pentecost,
the knight goes forth from Carduel
in poverty of heart,
again with lion and ally bird
he is woven into the one motif,
braided hand and claw
while the bird hurls over the carnage
and the battle-light flashes,
the pattern-welded blade
scrolled like the sea
is quenched in dragon sweat.

Now the bird sings something in French,
the horse shakes its belled harness,
and the hero rides home.

And now the lion mourns
his master's death,
couchant on the sepulchre
where these runes are cut:
Regard the tomb
of the strong king
who slew the dragon

as if to chide the reader
for dreaming he
might otherwise elude
what a king could not.

But the carver's own art
belies the inscription—

in the large roundel below
he's lavished
his most intricate care
on the worm itself.

There, the labyrinth of the dragon's torso,
its reptile ivy, continues to writhe,
linked somites of snake and bird,
and at each compass point a bestial mask—
a body lost in its own extravagance,
like the mutant spirals of life itself.

The hero kills what the artist
in love with creation
raises up again—

the spectre of the human heart,
that revenant unable to die.

3

Paul, the things we love mock us
with their lack of memory,
all but art
and that only
if the form suffices
and the maker's intelligence.

In answer to your death
and our old argument,
I've summoned
an ambiguous image
to satisfy us both—

the old man poking the fire
and fiercely shouting,
"Art must serve to lighten
life's vicissitudes;
the poet is a moral creature
as well as a maker."

And the boy I was replying,
"The artist's eye
is cold as any raptor's."

"Übermensch," you scoffed.
"The poem is human."

Then the third party
of our conversation, the sea
raking the gravel beach below,
no doubt spoke
to our separate convictions.

4

I don't know
if this answers
our old debate.
                                The man
working in the still room
with the light off the glacier
and the light off the sea
his sole apprentices—

he is deaf to inquiry.
Christian, he might say
art is a portion
of the Logos
and, therefore, good.

(Though he loved the dragon
and how it taxed
all he knew or guessed
of wood and metal,
that wouldn't be false.)

It has to do with memory,
efficient structure,
a vessel to carry the human breath,
carefully fitted with struts and timbers and

overlapping strakes,
caulked with tarred moss, wool,
whatever's at hand,
so as to keep
its little cargo safe.

Or like this door
whose deep incisions
centuries of ice and wind
off the East Fjords
could not erase—
memory scored the wood
to make it sing.

5

All day I have sat
on a dry river terrace
thinking of the Icelandic door
and of your death.

Kingbirds with their
pale yellow breasts
come to our garden,
and snakes,
of most formal and intricate design,
coil in the burning screes.

Inland three hundred miles
and several years,
I have listened
while the tide pushes
up the beach, and furrows it,
and leaves
some torn frond
of sea-lettuce, rootless
grey rag of itself,
and we argue
to no purpose,

entrenched in our convictions
as the sea.
                    And I think
of Arden waiting
in the empty house
and you in your blood
under the alder
soaking the small leaves,
the thirsty duff.
And I think of your son
blowing his trumpet
over the grey water,
and try to answer
the old question
the carver could ignore
being certain of God
as we are not.

You that took stock
with a caring heart,
and, past seventy,
had exhausted nothing
of your old joy
in walks by the ocean—
Paul, you said the poem
should raise us up in kindness and humanity.
And I,
older by this news of your violent death,
agree.

The Human City

Overwhelmed by images, I go walking the human city,
the swart harbor where buoys swing on their chains and clang
at the silted mouth, the cormorant-ridden, hungry water.
Women hurry past, gaunt women avid as gulls, wearing rings
at throat and wrist. Some are young and daub their cheeks with ocher
while others compose a griefless mask of gaiety.

Trumpets sound in the tall dusk of the streets—
so the Governor summons his own
to the pleasance. Dark wine he serves from the Levant,
a scarlet dish of berries, roast swan in almond sauce.
The ladies must adore his appetite, the feral sharpness of his gaze,
the falcon quickness of his fingers. Some he will admit
to his superb collection—his jewel-precise van Eyck,
his Veronese of the gods at sup, his beaten mask of Agamemnon.
His science is the self-possession of a perfect scrutiny.
Owning this hill, he owns the planet.
They pass the chestnut whose creamy flambeaux are like sea-foam
and the sailor on shore-leave—the strangely wooden equestrian of space,
his sea-widened eyes horizonless—rides a gibbet.
Hautboys and brazen horns shrill from the pillared house,
one shield-like window catches the sun,
and stones flush as if alive.

A bird-thin Boat girl, lame in one leg, picks through trash.
Eyes averted, I walk on past jewellers with portcullis doors—
icy diamonds, gold braided like girls' hair, a freckled mess of garnets—
beyond an ivy courtyard where linnets stir in the lance-shaped leaves
and one brittle shade is a map to the kingdom of loess and wind.
Each tenant hoards his life like the zinc coinage of the last war
and I walk on past limed pilasters of the vacant hippodrome,
past warehouses and silos and railroad sidings,
past mounds of coal from the rifled Basin,
and canneries whose scaled catwalks resemble a talus
of schist and mica—and so until the intertidal.
There, by the ringed quay, they set him at the last,
in his ship, the King who talked with birds,
and put torch to resinous pine—fire leaped

the mast-tree, blossoming the shroud, soldering
vizor to skull, and he was gone. After came swift incursions,
plague and man-geld, millennial witch-hunts,
and the heroic vellums used as boot leather—
the phase some called the Holy Ghost's
but was only the interregnum of history—
the Governor entertaining on his stony tor,
the swill town where immigrants fester and quicken
on the landfill, and barracks are jerrybuilt
over the tideland, while each generation the troops
are from more alien country.

Tonight as always the river crawls seaward
through a labyrinth of channels and sands marked by lightships.
The tidal mouth smells of salt and discarded bandages,
as if the wide dark estuary were a hospital serving the human city.
And I, in the feeding hour of the grebe,
in moonlight hung half visible
to sculpin and minnow, in the one dilation of the belled
mouth, say the old song that runs like this—

you indifferent mother of images, maker of coral
and our wayfaring sea flesh reeking of exile,
flint-hearted violent begetter of guilts and vendettas,
these salt-ribbed atolls of grief, come toward us
a little, we creatures so sorrowing, so fretful.
Say love for once. Say love will outlast the blood-rimmed
continents, the insomniac bones. Say love this once
will close our eyes in human sleep and children this night
will not catch cold in their trundle beds. Say this,
then go your way, old mother. I will follow.

By Indian River, Baranof Island

Keep this place in mind,
the peace you came to, pausing here
by Indian River. The water green
as absinthe, the thundering
so like silence.

                    Think of birds
you saw, or heard—the dipper
balancing on a stone
before it entered the stream,
the easy torrent of song
released from the throat of a wren.
You have come to admire
a music that isn't human
and here, it's everywhere
in leaf, bird, and falling
water. Something other
than our own—
the inexplicable greenness
of these deep pools—
and yet analogous
to the mind's clearest impulse.

In the Middle of Life

To an Actor Friend at 44

So it did not happen
you played the great roles,
suffering Tiresias
as you went your dogged way
to damnation. And Marie,
who briefly played your wife
off-off Broadway,
remains Hermione
locked in marble, the unswept snows
of twenty winters.

It did not happen you played Hamlet,
though you were well enough equipped
to brandish a rapier
and declaim brave, ambiguous things
from the battlements.

Now you stuff your heavy carcass
in a Kroger bearsuit, somnambulate
through industrial films,
do take after take of glamor shots
of bun with ketchup.

Sometimes, Richard, I think the gods
are small and mean.
They maim us in our dreams
before they give the coup de grâce.

For you had all the gifts in excess—
fine voice and eye,
expressive face, beauty.
I'll never forget, how, at twenty,
playing Pizarro in *The Royal Hunt of the Sun*,
you lost your lines
and how, without pausing,

you launched into lapidary doggerel,
a wild pastiche of Luis de Góngora

and Hugo Ball—of buds
popping open and light flaring
on crocus-colored peaks.

The Inca was speechless
and you beautiful as a god
in your breastplate and burnished helm,
your conquests all before you.

At Culver Hospital

A sense of the edge
recedes. The wistful intensity
with which you watched
certain clouds, those high
burnished thrones
that are the mountains
of western Indiana.

You come back into your body
little changed, after all.
You vomit some mucus,
hiccup, find it hard to piss.
Now you're awake
at 2 A.M. with a shattered
wrist. The "Just-Rite" sign
glows a dull sulfur
across 231. Vaguely,
like some old guilt,
your left hand begins to ache.

For awhile, you thought
you stood at the crossroads,
the great cathedral
hoisting its red bell
clangorous in the dawn.
Never again would you be
craven or undisciplined.
Pilgrim, you lie on your back,
your outstretched, swaddled arm
an atrophied wing. The drive
toward gnosis fizzles,
and you buzz for some codeine.

Walt Whitman at the Patent House

Walt Whitman has just visited the wounded Union
soldiers in the makeshift hospital at the Patent House.
Now he saunters out into the lilac-scented darkness.
He spies the moist half-moon and Venus about to set.
He has declaimed *Romeo and Juliet* to a blond amputee
from Pinkham's Notch and held a boy with head wounds
in the midst of his convulsions—heard the shrill cry
and saw those curious seizures, as of an amphibian
struggling back to the sea. Avid for death and the mysterious
nudity of bodies in death, he has gone from bed
to bed as an herbalist might—stooping, gentling,
inspecting, speaking words of encouragement.
The close air held the heavy sweetness of lilacs,
though more cloying, as if flowers steeped
in urine and blood could somehow preserve their sweetness.

From the White House, a sentry calls out
to his comrade and a mockingbird in the ravine
sings like a roisterer who cannot keep his tune.
A black coachman passes in a phaeton.
South, creekbeds of the Rappahannock are choked
with virile undergrowth and the tormentose
faces of the recent dead. He imagines a tomb
grander than the Capitol, a tomb like the grotto
of Tristan and Isolde, where all the green recruits
of the Union will lie together in their wounds.
He would gladly spend eternity in such a place,
in grieving adulation of the heroic dead.

Aubade

If, toward dawn, we wake and kiss
and with the cardinal crying sharply,
we do a sort of swimming
into the waters of ourselves,
no one will be wiser,
except us in the ways of love.
Ian sleeps and Allouez sleeps
but for the flabby jogger
in his Green Bay sweats,
the St. Norbert girl doing aerobics.
Ah, love, there are better ways
of staying in shape, even at 40.

So come again, darling, knock
at my door, as I will yours.
Forget the rowing machine,
the weights at the wrist;
even the cobra, the plough
can't open the chakras
like our tao. So let's do it
again and again, the good old dance
we always do, the sweet pumping
of something much softer than iron
toning our finest motor skills.

Remember, love, that story of Parzival?
After all the business of the Grail—
the melees and skirmishes and catechisms—
he meets, in a pavilion by the river,
his lady Condwiramurs of the white throat.
I can tell you it wasn't hunting cranes
with falcons, nor racing headlong on fallow
mares, they did (nor any knightly exercise).
But in each other's arms they found the cup
and drank in joy. Like all lovers
at first light, they were as two swans
waking in the reeds and gliding out,
their dazzling tracks converging on the sun.

Musée de Vieux Salauds

How much they exasperate us,
those arrogant old masters
toiling late in their platonic towers,
transmuting the brass farthings of experience
into Nobel prizes,
while, downstairs, their wives did the real work.
They never knew
diddly about chafed bottoms or scraped knees.
Pacing the battlements and gazing over the storm-beaten
acreage of their patriarchal hearts,
how could they remember
a child's birthday? Or stoop to kiss
a bruised toe, much less
fold a diaper? Unsoiled as the angelic
orders, they were above it all,
those brooding symbolistes.
For the chiseled ivory of a poem,
a century or two of fame,
they bartered their wives and children.
So now they seem to us like imperial
ocean-liners, steaming off toward the Indies
with their amethyst portholes ablaze,
their mosaic dancing floors, colossal
Bösendorfers, while ignored
in their nurseries, the babies wail
for the absent fathers, those arrogant old bastards.

Bathing Ian

Now the water's hot and deep enough,
the bath chair in place, I'll go
pull off his t-shirt and diaper

and lift him in my arms
who's so slight and yet so difficult
to hold. As if a hidden wind

skews him, his head jerks back.
I elbow the door open
and kneel by the steaming tub.

Shrieking, squealing, he's
ecstatic as I latch the velcro
strap across his chest,

the birth-scar over his left nipple.
I cinch the shorter straps
around each thigh, careful

of the little sac floating there,
his uncircumsized sex. *If
there were another way, Ian,*

I say under my breath. He grins
as if it were perfectly natural
for a father to bathe his ten-year-old son.

I squeeze the shampoo
into his thick blonde hair,
massage the skull familiar as my own,

rinse. Tilting back his head,
he laughs, it feels so good
when tight muscles can finally loosen.

I wash the open, vulnerable planes
of his back, the shoulderblades'
fretwork of blue veins, then ease him

into the chair again. Somehow,
for just a second, I'm holding
my own child-self, that very sequence

of DNA and ecstasy,
before I recollect myself
and the helpless boy under my hands.

I soap the washrag, scrub
the narrow chest, the slats of the belly
sharply etched as an athlete's,

the thighs twisting inwards,
calves, insteps. And now the tender
sex he's so seldom touched, I

wash, thinking a father's thoughts.
Awkwardly, I finish
with the nether parts, then say,

"We're done, Ian. Do you want to soak?"
"Yes," he speaks eagerly
with his eyes, the way we first

divined his intelligence.
I lean back against cool tiles,
close my eyes. How often

I would ask that my hands
fill with light. I imaged his body
as wind-broken krummholz

become the straight tree in the green meadow.
But desire, however desperate,
doesn't suffice or all children

would be well. I ready the towel
to receive him, then gather up
over my shoulders, the full slippery weight

of my son. I know I can't hold him
too much longer, nor ever entirely
let him go.

Petition

He's gone again.
We call and call to him,
but nothing cuts through
the static. A seizure
twists his neck to the left
toward the closet light,
pulls his mouth back
in a rictus, a sidelong
wolf grin. Panic

hurls us seven years
back to Nespelem,
to that trailer on its terrace
buffeted by a cold wind,
to that couple counting
the salaams of their infant son.

Now I'm strapping him
in his seat, crouching
in humid Indiana darkness,
the garage cluttered with
wheelchairs, therapeutic ladders, prone
standers like jurors
deliberating a hard case.

And now I'm gunning the engine
toward Culver Hospital,
the shot of valium, the inevitable
vomiting. Stroking his knee,
I race through stop
signs, past the safely darkened
houses of Market Street,
the municipal softball diamond,
where, under floods, the game
has gone into extra innings.

I ask whatever might be
listening at this late hour

that my son win back
his mind as he has before,
that tomorrow we carry
him home to this strict
life. I ask only
for the ordinary, no more.

After a Line by Antonio Machado

Through the doorscreen—
the taunts of laughing children,
chatter of grackles
settling down to roost.

At the edge of the woods,
fireflies appear.
They drift
over darkening lawns.

My children are gone from the house.
I can almost remember a life
I could call my own.

In solitude, a man ceases
to live among mirrors,
Antonio Machado wrote somewhere.
That widowed professor
would gladly have suffered
his child-wife, but his path
took him
through empty Soria countryside.

I open the door
and go out on the porch,
as years ago, after supper,
I would study
the night water,
the small waves
lapping the drift logs below.
After the traffic thinned
on the coastal road across Hood Canal
and the windows of the shore houses
winked out,
I was alone. Alone
with the unquiet water,
the moon tinkering
with its pewter.

So Machado along the Duero
found coplas of the true
Castillian earth. Even this
dry branch at the end of Main Street
fills with stridulous insects.
They can call a man
from the middle of his life
to that edge of dark elms,
to that tideland
where the boat is moored
with a loose slip knot,
and the plankton light
their small torches
as the random currents take them.

Grace

After Eugene Smith's Portraits of the Minamata Victims

This is not
Lafcadio Hearn's Japan—
elfin girls in silk kimonos,
flowering sprays embroidered with finches,
delicate feet
in snowy tabi,
"giving a mythological aspect—
the white cleft grace
of the foot of a fauness."

This is not that garden
where the human obliges the sun.
This is Shinobu,
whose mother, unknowing,
ate poisoned fish
and so damaged her fetus.
They wear the shame of deformity,
though guiltless.

In her long, dark schoolgirl's
dress, Shinobu
limps with a twisted,
pigeon-toed intensity.
Likewise, her hands
never quite obey—
strong desire
only contorts them.
To write, she learns
the trick of squinting.
Yet the camera
has truly caught
the awkward grace of adolescence,
a young girl's wounded radiance.

And there is the Shiranui Sea
where the laboring fathers
haul the well-tarred nets

daggered with small fish.
Who could have known
the water's contagion?
The quicksilver shoals,
corrosive metals,
Chisso had released?
(The company paid indemnities
to keep the people quiet.)

And this is Tomoko.
See! Her mother bathes her
in a deep tub, cradles
her curving spine in the crook
of her arm. How sweetly
she gazes down on the jutting
mouth, the foreshortened
brow, toward which the eyes
roll. How handsome
the mother's kerchiefed head,
her act of attention!

Please, do not turn away!
Hell is an aversion
to what is here.
And a simple photograph—
a woman bathing
her injured daughter—
can suggest those walls removed
from the twelfth century churches
of the Ile-de-France,
the sudden efflorescence
of stained glass
where stone had been,
the light falling
on neglected surfaces.

The Archer

Strapped in his wheelchair,
unable to navigate the damaged circuits
of his nerves, my son
has a Viking's heart.
In another time, another body,
there might have been a ship for him,
and a sea grey enough, and wide,
with a granite coast.
                                        But at this time,
in his present body, he cannot work the oars,
and the ship, anyway, is rudderless.

Now his neck twists
in the old reflex, his right fist
comes up to his mouth
and his left arm sweeps back
as if drawing the string of an invisible bow.

He seems like a figure
in a child's book of the constellations,
that archer of late summer skies.
And I am like an astronomer then
studying a nebula,
a swirling cowlick of stars,
as if his name were a string of numerals
in the catalogue of galaxies.

We're so remote, my son and I,
there's nothing on this mountaintop
but the dome of the telescope's eye
and the incalculable distance of God.

Moon Ode

Tonight I slipped out to the spa
we use for Ian's therapy
and took with me some cheap red wine
and drank while I watched you rise,
bathing the planet in mutability.
I lifted my glass to you, lovely sister,
and to my gumshoe friend, John Straley,
stalker of Baranof tidelands, detective
of dissolving identities, I drank.

O, I drank until I saw you calve,
your twin slipping like a narwhal
from your side. I thought of your whiteness
falling on the great sycamores of Sugar Creek
and into the cornfields west of town,
their blades creaking in the humid night.
What did those gnomic old Saxons say,
"Better to drink than to think overmuch"?

Was my father such a hero, drinking himself
numb, seeing how your whiteness
overwhelms everything? How was it with him
when he wrapped the scalding hotpacks
around my wasted legs? And now my son
with his fine clear eye and blighted
brainstem. Time to lift the glass again,
time to take my medication.
"Oh, my darlin', Oh, my darlin' Clementine,"
Dad would croon that dreadful ballad.

But I have always been a swimmer.
As a lifeguard, I pulled several children
from Sleepy Hollow Pool and set them on their feet.
One, I remember, thought I had delivered him
from certain drowning—in water
that came to his chin. An ocean roared
when Ian was born and the doctors
huddled on the shore. Now I am always

at sea, unable to tear my eyes
from the water, for fear another will go down.

John, the corn goes silver as the windy
straits beyond Sitka, and I am almost adrift
in the foam. A pod of humpbacks
surfaces with a sigh, blowholes venting
plumes of vapor. You told me of a sea-captain
who pieced together the wreckage
of his acts, and so faced them whole,
again, somehow.

Burro

Around the ring they go,
my son on his golden appaloosa
slumped over the saddle horn.
A therapist flanks him
on each side, and he is led
by a husky woman who is the calf-
roping champion of New Mexico.

They ask him to raise his head
but his head, though small,
is too heavy for him, and the reins
slip from his hands. Ambushed
by the old bitterness, I turn
from the barn. Past the corral
where a palomino colt trots stiffly
like a child practicing on stilts,
I plunge onto a rutted path
up among prickly pear and spindly
cholla, seeing little but my hobbled
feet, and the blind, determined ants
scavenging in the sun.

What might I have done with these years
spent lifting, changing, bathing
that helpless boy, my son? Even these
rickety cholla can haul a load
of purple blossom up from gutted
soil, but I want silence to water
my roots, days slowly sifting down,
accumulating like leaf fall in a cold lake.
Then the work might come.

As if a strap were tightening
around my chest, I turn back.
The patient group has emerged
from the barn and toils up
the slope toward me. His blond
head is up, he holds it

level for a second, and catches
my eye: grasping the reins,
my son is grinning with all he can
do. Suddenly, I find myself
laughing at my vacillation, how I
twist and turn from the given.

A father is a kind of donkey.
He has two heavy panniers
strapped to his shoulders.
They are filled with gold dust
and he dare not spill any.

A Familiar Song
November 1993

My son's inconsolable weeping
over the monitor tonight
seems like an old song
he's picked up listening in the November darkness,
adding his own lament to the ragged tune.
But I'm tired of the burden.
I just want to sleep
and so I let him cry
with that histrionic intensity
I can hardly abide.

This evening in the *Times*,
I saw photos of the beautiful, arched bridge,
Stari Most, "a crescent moon in stone,"
shattered by Croat guns.
I read how the architect, Hayrudin,
braced the limestone blocks with iron
and how lovers, crossing there
century by century, wore them smooth.

And still Ian cries, gulping the close air
like a gaffed fish, choking himself.
I know his braces aren't too tight,
and he's warm, his bear tucked
under his arm. He just wanted to say the lines
of the Old Green Grasshopper, for Christ's sake,
for once he wanted to speak his own part in the play
from his inarticulate body.

So he weeps, and I think of that other picture—
of the wide-eyed schoolchildren lying on cots
in the morgue of Kosevo Hospital.
They're just his age, nine maybe ten,
like the fifth graders who played the Centipede,
the Spider, and the Earthworm tonight.

Soon, very soon now, I'll go to him
and massage his tight shoulders.
I will lift him up in my arms
and tell him, "It's all right."
And he, with the ancient Grasshopper's wisdom,
will let me lie and console him.

Coda

After a Painting by Diego Rivera

1

Imagine!
A man bent double by flowers—
great, open-throated calla lilies, no less.
Ah, the burdens of poetry.

2

So it was one afternoon
when she came by
with her white shoulders all bare,
I was brought to my knees by beauty

and try as I might
I can never rise in this life again.

3

Into that wilderness of sorrows
I have walked a few paces
following the man of thorns,

but have gone no further
these several years.
I can believe his suffering,
the spikes, the hard blows
as if they were laying track with his body
into the twentieth century.

His release, I can't believe.
Why can't we admit
the project of love
broke him
as it would you or me?

Okanogan String Band Music

She's an Omak girl,
works evenings at KFC,
but when she strums her dulcimer and sings,
"I am a pilgrim and a stranger,"
your soul sets out with a rucksack
into the real Okanogan.

Hunched over a bit, short-winded,
but carried by her music,
the soul travels over sage terraces,
coulees choked with hackbrush,
ridges pale as dust. Horn Hill
trails into mist, Tunk Mountain
lies wholly in darkness. Now her friend
the veteran digs the spoons from his hip pocket
and clicks their silver heels, a boy not fifteen
thumps a beer can—"Hard, ain't it hard, good Lord,
to love one who never will be true"—
they belt out Guthrie in a bitter ecstasy.

Deeper into the Okanogan now,
into cool stands of timber, into lodgepole
thickets, the soul journeys, then down
into the valley of the Sanpoil.
Past the charred storefronts of Republic,
the café where you had pie and coffee once
and deliberated over something as innocent
as the baby's name. That was before
it all happened, before you understood
Aristotle, such terms as "peripety"
and "recognition." In the fire's aftermath,
tough spikes of mullein have taken root,
and the more delicate yarrow.

Swaying, eyes shut, the girl sings.
"Sometimes I feel like a motherless child,"
and the soul believes her. It knows a road
runs north past Nighthawk, climbs a notch

in the treeless mountain, descends
without fanfare into another country,
a democracy more perfect than ours.
But an ancient pain drags at the soul.
South, the valley of the Nespelem opens out
into meadows of sweet grass
and reservation kids learn rage
with their geography. The soul
has some business there
about a life unrealized, a boy
who describes himself as like "a bonzai
tree, small and twisted"—your son
born to these dry ridges, gasping for breath,
hemorrhaging in his right hemisphere.
Here on the Rez, history is congenital.
It inscribes itself in living tissue,
so much heartlessness and a little oblivion.

All the while, the girl has been singing,
willow-slender in her long white shift.
Her ballad is an ambush.
It is not about solace, the sweet release
of bodies coupling,
but the endless catechism of seeing
precisely what is here.

Now the Okanogan String Band winds up its show,
a second guitar, some old geezer blowing on a jug,
a jew's harp twanging like a crazed cicada,
and the vet's ruined voice begins, "There were twa
sisters sat in a bower . . ." and the dulcimer
goes still, and the guitars, the spoons, the jug.

The one voice must do it all,
the cracked voice of the poem must carry you
deep as nighthawks plummeting.
It sings broad mountains and towns of corrugated tin,
it sings the derelict communes of Aeneas Valley,
and children playing hide and seek
in the singed grasses of Tonasket.

It sings them all back home,
in the clear voice of the boy
who did poorly in geography,
in the rasping cadence of the man
who learned by heart the place names
of Southeast Asia. The veteran stands there
like a man who sets himself on fire
for a hopeless cause. He gives himself over
entirely to his song. And you receive it,
this potlatch of his solitude, this poor harp
he's made of his breastbone.

Only then does he release you
to your lonely American reliquary.

The Project

This is a song
for the rain, the cool rain
after the August drouth.
With its mouth wide open,
the earth sleeps
and the crickets continue to sing
under the cannas.

I have no ambition
but to lie on the sofa and dream
of the woolly bear caterpillar
I saw this morning
munching on a sunflower leaf.
It cares nothing
for the terrors of metamorphosis.
Sleeping, it will pass through the great changes.